D1255846

SHAME AND GUILT

SHAME AND GUILT

A Psychoanalytic and a Cultural Study

Gerhart Piers and Milton B. Singer

Foreword by Roy R. Grinker

W · W · NORTON & COMPANY · INC · NEW YORK

BF
575
.S45
P5

Library of Congress Catalog Card No. 76-140756
SBN 393 01082 1
1 2 3 4 5 6 7 8 9 0

CONTENTS

(5)

Contents

FOREWORD

SHAME AND GUILT have been loosely used interchangeably, although each stands for feelings derived from special early experiences that have influenced different psychological forces. Each is associated with a different intrapsychic pattern and probably contributes to a characterological type. An understanding of these differences is necessary for the development of adequate therapeutic procedures for the sick individual and for the accurate analyses of cultures.

The combination of psychoanalytic and anthropological contributions to understanding of the same phenomena is particularly fitting in the discussion of shame and guilt anxiety. Both are instilled in varying proportions in individuals by the forces of their culture through pressures and sanctions imposed on quantitatively susceptible energy systems; in turn the resulting character structures accrete to the cultural attitudes of the next generation. Such a transactional circular process is of great significance in this age of increasing mastery of the physical world, the results of which are utilized by the irrational forces of human nature and increase man's anxieties.

The bewildered focus of an attack to produce a change in humans—a lessening of all forms of overcompensatory aggressiveness—is the American mother who has been badgered by child-guidance mentors, first in the direction of rigid scheduling and now in permissive "self-demand." However, our culture puts a premium on achieving through competition to be, or to have, the best, which is conducive to internal shame or an external sense of inferiority, and at the same time imposes moral, religious, and filial responsibilities which result in a sense of guilt. Each secondarily leads to reactions, defensive against personal anxiety, but aggressive or masochistic within the social group. In what manner may this circular process be altered—it matters not whether through social change, altered child rearing, or treatment of individuals—is an important question implied by this timely and scholarly monograph.

Roy R. Grinker

INTRODUCTION
to the Norton Edition

THIS REISSUE has been suggested to us by the continued interest in our statement about the double roots—individual and social—of the twin affects of shame and guilt. The first printing, published by Charles C. Thomas of Springfield, Illinois, in 1953, was soon exhausted, and so were two small private reprintings. Both authors resisted for a while the entreaties of their new publisher, who urged a new edition. Our hesitation was largely due to our feeling that in our respective fields, psychoanalysis and anthropology, findings and thinking —particularly concerning the phenomenon of "guilt"— have advanced in a measure that is not adequately contained within the frame of our original thesis. Nevertheless, we believe that our *Shame and Guilt* has played a sufficiently significant role in this very development to warrant its again being made available. We address this edition especially to the growing group of analysts and social scientists who, by learning from each other, attempt to deepen the understanding of Western man in his dealings with the world around him and the world inside.

The current edition is essentially a reprint of the 1953 original, with only minor changes in spelling and bibliography. We intend to follow up in due time with a full review of intervening developments and a somewhat revised statement of the authors' current view of the entire complex matter.

GERHART PIERS
MILTON B. SINGER

Chicago, September 1970

ACKNOWLEDGMENTS

I WISH TO THANK the following for reading Part I and for offering many valuable suggestions, some of which I could incorporate into the final draft: Dr. Therese Benedek, who also formally discussed Part I in its original presentation to the Chicago Psychoanalytic Society in November, 1950, and to whose encouragement I feel particularly indebted; Dr. Franz Alexander, whose earlier statement of the problem is used as the starting point for parts of my thesis; Miss Helen Ross, Dr. Paul Kramer, Dr. Elizabeth Zetzel, and Dr. Raymond De Saussure, the last three for their thoughtful discussions of my paper; Dr. Roy R. Grinker, who first suggested publication in the present form and who offered many helpful criticisms and suggestions; Dr. Eduardo Weiss; and last but not least, I want to thank my wife, Dr. Maria Piers, who contributed greatly to

Acknowledgments

this study, particularly from her knowledge and experience in child development and anthropology.

GERHART PIERS

I am indebted to Professor Robert Havighurst of the University of Chicago for his kindness in making available to me his unpublished studies of American Indian children.

MILTON B. SINGER

PART I / BY GERHART PIERS

Shame and Guilt

A Psychoanalytic Study

One

GUILT AND SHAME

OF ALL THE more organized forms of intrapsychic tension, those manifested in the feelings of *guilt* and *shame* are possibly the most important ones, not only in emotional pathology, but quite generally in ego development, character formation, and socialization. Although they have been recognized in their importance by the great majority of modern psychologists, it is quite surprising to find that they are usually neither clearly differentiated nor adequately defined. This is particularly true for the feeling of *shame*, its phenomenology, genetics, and dynamics.

In order to delineate both concepts, it seems advisable to start with the more largely accepted views held in regard to *guilt* feelings. Briefly stated, they are: The dynamically important sense of guilt remains as such unconscious, although the concomitant anxiety becomes conscious. The sense of guilt is generated by the superego. Without the formation of such an internal authority, psychological "guilt" does not occur. (For brevity's sake, we shall in the following frequently say "guilt" instead of "guilt feelings" or "sense of guilt," a semantic inaccuracy for which common psychoanalytic usage pleads legitimacy.) Guilt must not be confounded with apprehension, which in the context of our particular interest is the proper designation of the "fear of being caught"; nor is the feeling of guilt the same as a conscious and realistic fear of impending punishment.

Guilt, then, is the painful internal tension generated whenever the emotionally highly charged barrier erected by the superego is being touched or transgressed. The transgressors against which this barrier has been erected are id impulses that range from aggressiveness to destructiveness. Most authors also include here sexual impulses, particularly those related to incestuous drives. The irrational punishment, the unconscious threat of which is held forth to the transgressor, is governed by the Law of Talion and consequently spells either complete annihilation or mutilation of the offending organ as carrier of the tabooed impulse. The psychologically most important anxiety contingent to the feeling of guilt is, therefore, the widely studied *castration* anxiety after which the entire punishment complex is usually named.

Accordingly we use here the term "superego" exclusively as stemming from internalization (introjection) of the punishing, restrictive aspects of the parental images —regardless of whether the original images corresponded to reality or were largely projections of the individual's own magical destructiveness. It may be stated here in an oversimplified fashion that no one develops a sense of guilt without a punitive parent image, the latter being based either on historical reality or projective imagination. For it has been shown that the projection of primitive destructive impulses and possibly fantasies into the parental images plays a large part in the formation of the superego. Since at an early developmental stage the primary narcissistic "belief" in the omnipotence of thought and wish prevail, the superego is automatically endowed with similar power.

From this brief summary, it will be clear that we do not hold the formation of the superego to be contingent upon the "passing of the Oedipus complex." The development of an internalized conscience with its executive arm of guilt feeling occurs prior to and in large portions independent of the oedipal situation. E.g., the importance of oral aggressiveness and the role of the mother as punitive agent have been amply demonstrated in this connection.

There seems to be a large body of agreement regarding the sense of guilt. Much less clarity obtains about the phenomena connected with shame. This confusion may be partly a semantic one since the word connotes different things to different people, and the shades of meaning vary in different languages.

In the following discussion, I shall deal with the phenomenon of shame in only *one* meaning, viz., that of a distinctly differentiated form of inner tension which as such is a normal concomitant of ego development and superego formation, at least in our culture. One can deal with shame also by regarding it as one of the many *affects*, in one category with rage, fear, hatred, love, hope, etc. Although I refer to shame occasionally as an "emotion," I wish to have it understood that the problems of affect psychology do not concern me here. Finally, shame is treated by many authors as a neurotic *symptom*, and used synonymously with bashfulness, shyness, self-effacingness, or as a *character trait*, like modesty. Although shame tension in the way I am using this term here underlies many of these symptoms or character defenses, this is not always the case, as I shall try to show.

The way in which Freud [1] used the term "Scham" originally makes it clear that he definitely was concerned with shame not as a symptom nor as affect but as a tension originating from what he later termed superego. However, shame to him is definitely related to sexuality, or rather to one particular aspect of it, viz., exhibitionism. This may have been, to a certain degree, semantically determined. The German "Scham" and "Schamgefuehl" almost immediately suggest a specific emotion connected with the exposing of the nude body, particularly the genitals. The genital region is called "die Scham," pubic mound, "Schamberg," pubic hair, "Schamhaare," etc.*

* Whereas the adjective "schamhaft" still carries the connotation of "shielding one's genitals," "schamlos," literally "devoid of the sense of shame," is frequently used in the sense of "ruthless," i.e., lacking a sense of guilt.

Thus, in *Three Contributions to the Theory of Sex*, Freud uses the term "Scham" in close connection with "Ekel" (loathing, disgust), at times almost synonymously with it and defines it as "the force which opposes the voyeuristic drive and might be overcome by the latter. . . ."[2] In the same treatise, shame, together with loathing, is described as one of the barriers against the sexual drive, erected during latency as a product of training. Freud follows this definition with a strange afterthought: "Actually this development is organically determined, fixated by heredity and it is established occasionally entirely without the help of training." He emphasizes this statement for which he gives no further evidence by the hard-to-translate flourish: "Training . . . merely follows the lines primarily drawn by the organic, making them clearer and deeper."[3]

It is difficult to conceive of shame, disgust, and esthetic and moral judgments as being established without the influence of early educational factors. The story of Adam and Eve reflects the general belief that "natural man" does not know shame (or guilt). It may be that Freud had in mind either physiological concomitants of the affect of shame, e.g., blushing or instinctive (inborn) behavior patterns of flight or hiding. This, then, would be along lines that Darwin had pursued in his investigation of emotional expressions.[4] Although shame, to be manifestly expressed, has to draw on such primitive reflexes and patterns as does any psychological phenomenon, it seems to be very questionable to consider the *feel-*

ing of shame as being determined by them. In any case, the above passage reflects Freud's awareness of the early developmental roots of shame.

Nunberg [5] merely restates Freud's position in regarding the feeling of shame as a reaction formation against exhibitionism, and any other not directly sexual form of shame as derived from the former.

Fenichel describes shame in two rather disparate ways. In one place, shame, for him, is ". . . the specific force directed against urethral-erotic temptation. *Ambition*, so often described as an outcome of urethral-erotic conflicts, represents the fight against this shame." Pride in controlling the urethral sphincters is deemed to arise from the fact that in bladder training the child is usually "put to shame," much more so than in bowel training.[6] It should be noted that Fenichel describes here "urethral ambition" as reaction to humiliating training experiences rather than as derivative from pride in urethral achievement (in boys). In another place Fenichel,[7] evidently closely following Freud's earlier statement, refers to shame as a defense mainly against exhibitionism and scoptophilia, "not simply (a special form) of castration anxiety . . . but a more specific feeling . . . undoubtedly also rooted in a primitive physiological reflex pattern." "Being ashamed of oneself," he counts under the heading of guilt.

Norman Reider, in the discussion of a quite unusual "case of shame," [8] follows Fenichel in all essentials although he admits that "the nature of the reflex physiological pattern is not at all evident," and also points out that shame might be utilized by some as a defense against a more intolerable sense of guilt. Erik H. Erikson, in his recent work,[9] gives expression to a similar thought: "Shame is an emotion insufficiently studied because in our civilization it is so early and easily absorbed by guilt." This author distinguishes between these two tensions very clearly and ascribes their respective onset to different stages of development. However, he prefers to think of the *shame* impulse "to bury one's face, to sink into the ground" as "essentially rage turned against the self," which is an important *guilt* mechanism.

A clear exposition of the sharp and important difference between shame and guilt has been given by Alexander, first in a paper published in 1938, "Remarks about the Relation of Inferiority Feelings to Guilt Feelings" [10] and again in his *Fundamentals of Psychoanalysis*.[11] As indicated in the title of the first paper, the author at that time used the term "inferiority feelings" and not the more inclusive term "shame." For both semantic and psychological reasons, we prefer "shame" and regard "inferiority feelings" as concomitants and results of "shame" anxiety.*

A good example of both the greatly advanced un-

* We would also like to avoid the association with the "inferiority complex" popularized by Alfred Adler. Much as we recognize Adler as a pioneer in dynamic ego psychology, we cannot agree with his postulate that a sense of inferiority marks the beginning of ego development. The early infantile ego, for us, is characterized by omnipotence, a condition to which the later ego will regress under particular stress.

derstanding and the still remaining lack of clarity is found in this passage: ". . . in spite of the fact that in structural terms inferiority feelings and guilt feelings can be described with the same formula as a tension between ego and ego-ideal they are fundamentally different psychological phenomena, and as a rule their dynamic effect upon behavior is opposite." [10] It would seem almost imperative that emotions phenomenologically and dynamically so different would also differ structurally.

STRUCTURE OF SHAME

WE REALIZE then that most authors so far have considered shame a comparatively insignificant emotion or anxiety, more or less a result of conflicts over sexual strivings, usually in the particular form of exhibitionism. Only Erikson and Alexander ascribe to shame an importance equal to "guilt" in human pathology.

In the following I shall attempt to describe the differences between the two even sharper, both phenomenologically and dynamically.

To start with, I suggest, by way of definition, a structural description of shame which will then be discussed in more detail in the following chapters.

The following seem to me properties of shame which clearly differentiate it from guilt:

1) Shame arises out of a tension between the ego and the ego ideal, not between ego and superego as in guilt.

2) Whereas guilt is generated whenever a boundary (set by the superego) is touched or transgressed, shame occurs when a goal (presented by the ego ideal) is not being reached. It thus indicates a real "shortcoming." Guilt anxiety accompanies transgression; shame, failure.

3) The unconscious, irrational threat implied in shame anxiety is abandonment, and not mutilation (castration) as in guilt.

4) The Law of Talion does not obtain in the development of shame, as it generally does in guilt.

Several of the terms used here require further elaboration. An attempt will then be made to validate the entire thesis through observations of both normal and clinical phenomena.

Three

EGO IDEAL AND SUPEREGO

I HAVE SUGGESTED that shame represents a tension between ego and ego ideal, rather than between ego and superego. It seems immaterial whether one wishes to regard the ego ideal merely as one particular aspect of the superego or as a psychological formation entirely separate and independent from the latter. In *The Ego and the Id* (1923), Freud uses both terms interchangeably throughout. As is well known, he clearly describes them there as a "precipitate in the ego" from that sexual phase of development which was dominated by the Oedipus complex.[12] However, in a different passage he adds that the superego is also a result of the prolonged helplessness and dependency of the human animal. He points out the two-facedness of the superego which not only exhorts the ego to become like father, but also forbids it to attempt certain things which are father's prerogative. Freud feels that this state of affairs has derived from the formidable task to repress the Oedipus complex. To achieve this—in deference to the superego—the ego borrows strength from the father as Ideal.

It should be possible to arrive at a greater clarity about the function of the ego ideal as distinguished from the superego, since these two aspects of "superstructure" in the ego have different—at times opposing—integrative tasks, and their respective generic sources, too, can be differentiated.

First, the ego ideal appears to contain *a core of narcissistic omnipotence*. The amount of it is, of course, subject to tremendous individual variation. Needless to say that a "too-much" makes for a great variety of pathological conditions with overinflated, grandiose, or perfectionistic ideals that put the ego under unbearable tensions. But to maintain a minimum of primitive omnipotence seems to be necessary to establish such healthy, integrative functions as self-confidence, hope, and trust in others. Possibly it also requires a minimum of magic belief in one's invulnerability or immortality to make for physical courage and to help counteract realistic fear of injury and death.

Second, the ego ideal represents the sum of the *positive identifications* with the parental images. Both the loving, the reassuring parent, the parent who explicitly and implicitly gives the permission to become like him, and the narcissistically expecting parent and the parent who imposes his own unobtained ideals on the child may be represented here.

Third, the ego ideal contains layers of *later identifications*, more superficial, to be sure, and more subject to change than the earlier ones, but of the greatest social importance. The "social role" that an individual assumes in any given social situation is largely determined by the structure of these developmentally later parts of his ego ideal. There is a continuous psychological interchange between the individual ego ideal and its projections in the form of collective Ideals. It is important to recognize that the images that go into the formation of this part of the ego ideal do not have to be parental ones at all. The sibling group and the peer group are much more significant.[13]

Fourth, the ego ideal is in continuous dynamic interfunction with the unconscious and conscious *awareness of the ego's potentialities.* This part of the ego ideal must contain the *goals* of what has been variously termed "instinct of mastery" (Hendrick),[14] "mastery principle" (Fenichel),[15] etc. A better term for what I have in mind might be "maturation drive." It would signify a psychic representation of all the growth, maturation, and individuation processes in the human being, beginning with the most primitive organizational functions made possible by the progressive myelinization of the nervous system in infancy up to those highly complex functions that strive for what is somewhat romantically referred to as self-realization. As far as I can see, nobody has better envisioned the far-reaching meaning of the "maturation drive" (without naming it such) nor described it more beautifully than the phenomenologist, Erwin Straus, in an essay "Die aufrechte Haltung." [16] The successful exertion of this "maturation drive" in accordance with the ego ideal is accompanied by a sense of pleasure which Karl Buehler [17] has termed "Funktionslust"—the pleasure experienced in and through one's own well-functioning. This "lust" is of course essentially a "narcissistic," not a libidinous one, although sexual pleasure ideally combines both.

It will be clearer now why I prefer to use the more inclusive term "shame" rather than "inferiority feelings." The latter term implies comparison with external figures, hence does not quite express this completely internalized tension between ego and ego ideal. The two terms stand in somewhat similar relationship to each other as "guilt feelings" and "fear of punishment." Also, "inferiority feeling" does not well describe that particular inner tension which stems from failure to reach one's own potentialities.

It will be equally clear now that we mean by "shame" something quite different from "sexual shame." It is related to what Hegel must have had in mind when he wrote: "Shame does not mean to be ashamed of loving, say on account of exposing or surrendering the body . . . but to be ashamed that love is not complete, that . . . there still be something inimical in oneself which keeps love from reaching completion and perfection." [18]

Shame then occurs whenever goals and images presented by the ego ideal are not reached. If shame can reach such a degree that it appears as conscious anxiety it must imply a severe unconscious threat to the ego. This threat, however, is not the fear of the wrath of the parental images, or in other words, fear of annihilation or mutilation proferred as punishment by the superego under the Talion principle. Behind the feeling of shame stands not the fear of hatred, but the fear of *contempt* which, on an even deeper level of the unconscious, spells fear of *abandonment*, the death by emotional starvation. The parent who uses as educational tools the frequent exposure of the child's immaturity ("Look how foolish, dumb, clumsy you are!") will be the one to lay the foundation of such fear of contempt. We suspect, however, that the deeper-rooted shame anxiety is based on the fear of the parent who walks away "in disgust," and that this anxiety in turn draws its terror from the earlier established and probably ubiquital separation anxiety. (Some further discussion of the genetic problem of shame in Chapter 9.)

Withdrawal of love can be a threat only from positive images. It is as if the loved parental images or the projected power and life sustaining sources of one's own omnipotence threaten to abandon the weakling who fails to reach them. Accordingly, on a higher social and more conscious level of individual development, it is again not fear of active punishment by superiors which is implied in shame anxiety, but social expulsion, like ostracism. Fenichel was, therefore, right when he, although still assuming that shame was the specific reaction to scoptophilia, suspected that it was not just a fear of the "evil eye," i.e., a peculiar form of castration anxiety. Indeed, it is not the malevolently destructive eye, but the all-seeing, all-knowing eye which is feared in the condition of shame, God's eye which reveals all shortcomings of mankind.

GUILT-SHAME CYCLES

To accentuate the different dynamics of guilt and shame, it may be well at this point to repeat what has been said about their frequent antagonism. In this I follow generally Alexander's reasoning.

Take a male individual in whom sexual impulses mobilizing the Oedipal conflict arouse a (conscious or unconscious) sense of guilt. To avoid this conflict and its painful concomitant guilt anxiety, he either inhibits his sexuality entirely or permits only pregenital outlets or equivalents. Such behavior will bring him into sharp conflict with the accepted and expected behavior of his chronological or social peers. The resulting anxiety has clearly the character of shame. However, the shame tension in turn can be so painful that it might lead to overcompensatory behavior of, say Don Juanism. This brings him again back into the tabooed Oedipal sphere, giving rise to the feeling of guilt. Thus we have the cycle: sexual impulse → guilt → inhibition and/or regression → shame → sexual acting-out → guilt. The dynamic polarity of the two forms of anxiety is clearly demonstrated.

A very similar cycle obtains in the realm of *hostility*. It is an almost universal occurrence in our culture that impulses (or acts) of aggression generate a sense of guilt which results in their inhibition. This inhibition frequently spreads from destructiveness proper to assertiveness and in more pathological cases, to activity as such. The resulting passivity brings about a conflict accompanied by the anxiety signal of shame. Shame in turn might lead to overcompensatory aggressive fantasies or behavior, setting off the alarm signal of guilt. Thus a similar vicious cycle is established: Aggression → guilt → inhibition → passivity → shame → overcompensatory aggressiveness → guilt.

It may well be debated here whether the two cycles described are not actually dynamically identical. On at least one occasion (in *Civilization and its Discontents*), Freud [19] has clearly stated that he believes guilt proper to be generated exclusively by aggressive, and not by any other drives. "Sexual guilt," as mentioned above in connection with the first "vicious cycle" would then be subsumed under the aggressive-destructive aspect of the Oedipal conflict, i.e., the unconscious tendency to destroy the parental figure. Without further discussing it at this junction, I would like to question this standpoint. It would seem to me that in our Christian culture, whether under St. Paul's or Calvin's protectorate, a specific sense of guilt connected with seeking sensual-sexual *pleasure* is clearly discernible, particularly in women.

CHAPTER

Five

PATHOLOGY AND
PHENOMENOLOGY

THE "vicious cycles" of "guilt—shame—guilt" apply
to dynamic situations in flux, neurotic individuals floun-
dering between the horns of two powerful anxieties and
wavering in their choice of defenses and behavior. Such
pictures are not infrequently observed during the course
of a therapeutic analysis when defenses have become
mobile and resistance leads to either regression or acting
out. The usual clinical picture is a more static one. Here
the individual has made a choice and has settled for one
anxiety in order to avoid the other.

Take the case of the *moral masochist*. Haunted by
a deep-rooted and all-pervading sense of guilt, he contin-
uously attempts to buy off his sadistic superego by en-
during *shame*ful humiliation. There is no doubt that he
actually experiences shame with all its pain—were it not
so, he could not buy off his guilt. Yet shame, for him, is

evidently easier to bear than the primary guilt and, experiencing humiliation, he achieves temporary surcease from his conscience. In clinical practice, it is at times not easy to discern whether spontaneously expressed or analytically uncovered shame, shyness, self-debasement actually spring from a deep sense of inadequacy, or whether they represent frozen attitudes of atonement for an unconscious guilt.

Conversely, a situation of guilt with all its anxiety can be sought as a refuge from a pressing sense of shame. Compulsive misdemeanor accompanied by guilt anxiety and apprehension is frequently a method to hide the shame over the inability to enter adult relationships or do constructive work. *Pathological male exhibitionism* ("indecent exposure," forensically) is such an example. To describe it simply as a primary libidinous drive ("Partialtrieb") which manages to break through the physiologically predetermined barrier of shame is not doing justice to the much more intricate dynamic process. In fact, it seems a tautology to state that pathological exhibitionism in adults is simply due to a continuation (fixation) of a specific infantile drive—viz., exhibitionism. It is a most painful sense of shame over his inadequacy—centered usually on the size and function of the penis—that prompts the exhibitionist to do the forbidden aggressive act. The unconscious goal is the one that he ordinarily achieves: namely to *arouse* the onlooker; sexual excitement or fear and hatred in the woman passer-by, and physical attack from males, including not infrequently the so-called guardians of the law. The strange calm that the typical exhibitionist displays when he is being "worked over" at the police station indicates what is happening; a great momentary relief from his shame anxiety through the mere fact that he has been able to "arouse" the others. (The masochism which is so frequently connected with exhibitionism and which is simultaneously satisfied is secondary.)

The barrier which he actually had to overcome is not shame, but his sense of guilt (over aggression) which frequently is quite well developed too, the typical exhibitionistic offender being an otherwise law-abiding conformist citizen. To be sure, the above description does not take into account even deeper layers of the unconscious of both the voyeur and the exhibitionist. There one will find confusion about male-female, fantasies of the phallic mother and of the magic power of "seeing" and "being seen."

Another clinical situation in which feelings of guilt conceal a shame problem is the so-called *masturbation "guilt."* This is sometimes an early and easy discovery in the treatment of constricted or passive male characters. It is the usual experience that uncovering this "complex," even if it should occur quite dramatically in the therapeutic course, does not change the neurotic structure at all. The fact is that behind this façade of guilt, there is usually hidden a much deeper-seated problem of *shame* over sexual inadequacy and/or passive homosexuality, and only working on this brings further progress. (Reik mentions in his autobiography that masturbation gives rise to shame rather than guilt.[20])

An interesting and less obvious situation is sometimes encountered in the analysis of sexual disturbances in women, particularly *frigidity*. At a certain point it may happen that incestuous impulses and fantasies, particularly concerning the brother and brother figures, are uncovered and that the patient brings forth a great amount of self-accusatory confirmatory material proving to herself and the analyst how sexually "bad" she really is. It is then a not infrequent discovery to find beneath this layer of guilt the much more poignant difficulty of dealing with the patient's sense of shame over her imagined inadequacy. By claiming that she is a "bad girl," the patient conceals from herself that she cannot accept being a girl at all which to her means an ineffective or deprived being.

The foregoing implies that we should be more circumspect in using the term *"sexual guilt."* We should reserve this term only for the superego anxiety mobilized by infringements on the taboo on sensual pleasure, by collisions with the incest taboo, and by those situations in which sexuality and destructiveness are fused. Everything else will be more properly termed "shame," as it refers to the immature infantile elements connected with sex. The so frequently encountered connection of "sex" and "dirt" will most usually represent a problem of shame rather than guilt. Conversely, sexual shyness and modesty, usually subsumed under the heading of "shame," are not infrequently manifestations of true (unconscious) sexual guilt over forbidden impulses, exhibitionistic or otherwise.

A similar differentiation is in place for *"oral guilt"* and *"oral shame."* "Oral guilt" should refer exclusively to the anxiety brought about by the superego reaction to the depriving, demanding, parasitically destructive, cannibalistic, biting aspect of orality. The anxiety due to tension between ego ideal and the dependent, passive, suckling needs is better called "oral shame."

In this connection, a word about the affect of *envy* might be in place. We frequently find that it is held in suppression or repression due to a sense of guilt about it. This may be entirely correct if it refers to one particular form of envy which usually has its roots in an oral aspect of sibling rivalry and the unconscious syllogism of which reads something like this: "The other one is *receiving* more than I; I need to take it away from him by force or by killing him." This form of envy is usually accompanied by the affect of *resentment* which can be so strong that it determines the color of an entire personality. This resentment is, of course, directed against the parental image accused of being partial to the sibling, or against the projected image in the form of God or Fate. There is, however, a different form of envy, generically derived from the maturation process and non-oral aspects of competition with the parent and sibling, the unconscious syllogism of which is approximately this: "The other one is so much *bigger and better* than I am; I am so small, I can never reach him." This form of envy (invidi-

shame and with "beggar's pride" they display the defect as if it were an asset. More frequently, however, a more subtle dynamism underlies the phenomenon.

Theodor Reik has described the "blindly fleeing forward" as one of the characteristics of masochists.[22] These people don't seem to be able to stand the suspense anxiety of pending punishment and therefore quickly bring it about themselves. It seems to me that this unconscious attitude is particularly prominent in shame-induced "masochism," if masochism should be retained as the descriptive term. It is based on a peculiar narcissistic maneuver that prevents the defeat from being inflicted by others by bringing it about oneself. This maneuver preserves the narcissistic position of "I have really done it myself—I could just as well not have done it at all—nobody has really defeated me." Thus, when a man who is deathly afraid of being "made a fool of" acts particularly awkward in a test situation, this may be due to one of four conditions: it may be an actual paralysis of action through overwhelming panic; it may be due to an inhibitive sense of guilt that makes it impossible for him to succeed against parental or sibling figures; it may prove, on analysis, to be a compulsive repetitive acting out of a "rebellion through obedience" against a disparaging parent image, its syllogism being: "This is what you always said I would do— that I could not succeed—so I act in accordance with your contempt and lack of confidence—well knowing that I am hurting your pride and ambition." But in still other cases, the unconscious goal of this self-defeat was simply to "have it done myself—nobody has done it to me," or: "What the other one has seen was not a real deficiency after all, since it was manufactured by myself." Thus the real catastrophic shame is prevented. The clown who makes others laugh at himself never feels humiliated —since *he* has *made* them laugh.

A word here, too, about the role of the *anticipatory fantasy* in creating masochistic pain (anxiety). Its great clinical importance seems to have been largely neglected in the literature with the exception of some passages in Reik's book on masochism. The basic dread is that of the external event (catastrophe) which, coming without the individual's knowledge, timing, or control, questions the omnipotence to which the neurotic hangs on precariously. To assert this "omnipotence of thought," the neurotic will resort to "imagining the worst." This is unconsciously intended to prepare him magically against the shock—since he has "known it all along." However, this device frequently backfires. In the very assertion of magic omnipotent "thinking," reality testing is temporarily weakened. The imagined evil becomes nearly real itself and the anxiety which was meant to be prevented breaks through. As the German proverb says: "If you paint the Devil on the wall, he'll come." Originally, of course, the Devil was painted so he would *not* come—as *apotropeion*, the magic picture which keeps the ghosts away. I believe that many, if not all, compulsive phobias show this mechanism. Again, it can be more easily demonstrated in individuals with predominant shame problems. Their narcissism is more threatened and therefore is usually being "overprotected" in the fashion outlined above.

Seven

CHARACTER FORMATION

IT FOLLOWS from the foregoing that guilt and shame are: (a) clearly differentiated; (b) that one can lead to the other; and (c) that one can conceal the other. Considering this last point, it appears that certain personalities have developed a predilection for one or the other reaction pattern. Some seem to hide ingeniously their shame so that it appears as guilt, some become ashamed in situations to which others react with a sense of guilt, etc. Characterologically these predilections in the choice of anxiety are in more extreme cases so apparent that one would like to speak of *guilt-ridden* or *shame-driven* personalities, respectively.* The guilt-ridden person is held

* This is by no means intended to lead toward a true dynamic characterology. As far as I can see, most existing ones are based on a dichotomy of phenomena, and on closer investigation, reveal a division of characters into "A's" and "non-A's" rather than polarities. This seems to me the case, e.g., with Jung's character types. "Introversion" is a well-conceived entity, but extroversion is not much more than the absence of the former. Even true polarities, like hysterical-obsessive,

back, becomes constricted in his character, his earlier and subsequent identifications tend to be with unconstructive images, inactivity, passivity, or turning against the self are his fate. Guilt-engendered activity is at best *restitution* (sacrifice, propitiation, atonement) which rarely frees, but brings with it resentment and frustration rage which in turn feed new guilt into the system. The shame-driven individual has better potentialities as to maturation and progress. His primary identifications may be healthier to start with, his later identifications may permit him to proceed from the original images to siblings, peers, and broader aspects of the social environment. If his ambitious drive is coupled with creativeness, it may actually lead to a spontaneous curing of the original narcissistic wound. The guilt-ridden person introjects and expels ("extrojects"); the shame-driven identifies and compares. Whereas the shame-driven might be propelled beyond his natural limitations and break, the guilt-ridden as a rule will not even reach his potentialities.

are inadequate for a dynamic typology. Similarly, to look at human character from the standpoint of "choice of anxiety" is merely stressing one aspect, and not the deepest, for the purposes of clarification. To speak of people exclusively dominated by shame or guilt is, of course, an abstraction.

CHAPTER

Eight

THE QUESTION OF ONSET

THESE differences give rise to a question about the genetic roots of the two aspects of superego function. At what stage of ego development can they be first observed? That guilt feeling requires the formation of a superego has been said before, and consequently, it belongs to a comparatively late stage. The dynamic requisite for shame is merely that the process of ego-finding be under way. Shame has much to do with body function and body performance as such; guilt requires another object —that, too, speaks for a later development of guilt. Comparison with others and awareness of "inferiority" must occur quite early, most probably earlier than any guilt feelings can have developed.

This seems somewhat paradoxical in the light of what has been said about the effect of either emotion on symptom and character formation. It might need further careful direct observation of children to decide this issue.

(There does not seem to be any pertinent observation since an early paper by J. K. Friedjung.[23])

E. H. Erikson, in his comprehensive ego development scheme, sees the "danger point" for the formation of shame in the developmental stage of anal-muscular integration (approximately the second year of life). Shame (which Erikson links together with "doubt") is considered the specific obstacle in the task of first establishing what he terms "autonomy." This occurs prior to the genesis of guilt in the following stage of locomotor and genital ("phallic") development with its oedipal struggles. He also states succinctly: "Visual shame precedes auditory guilt." [9] Erikson is, however, well aware that these basic conflicts and anxieties have genetic roots in even earlier ("oral") phases of ego integration.

In discussing these problems, a number of experts on early development (E. Sylvester, H. Ross, and Th. Benedek) [24] have pointed out to me that shame must be based on that particular form of anxiety that comes about when the original unit with the mother is first broken, the child starts to walk away and to master the environment on his own. He has to learn how to depend on "long distance" directions from the parent conveyed through auditory and visual rather than through the more primitive contact senses. The important signals cease to arise directly from within the original mother-child unit, but come from another person, a "watcher" and "caller."

THERAPEUTIC CONSIDERATIONS

I T I S to be expected that a sharper clarification of guilt and shame will be important for a more effective therapy. An analytic episode might illustrate this.

A patient with a highly pathological propensity to lose his money in a spiteful, destructive way asks at the beginning of treatment to be permitted to pay me at the end of each session since he "cannot quite trust himself" to keep enough money for a monthly bill. After several months during which progress was made, this particular attitude was discussed in terms of the guilt feeling he would have to stand if he would deprive me of my money as he had done to his family and previously to his father, from whom he had stolen. I suggested that he could be trusted now to take the responsibility for a monthly bill. A distinct setback in the analytical progress can later on be definitely related to this incomplete analysis and premature "therapeutic acting." The patient was only slightly threatened by guilt over stealing from me; rather the act of paying me after each hour had become his method of "putting me in my place" as a hired hand, to assert his superiority as an employer in order to overcome a tremendous sense of inadequacy and invidious comparison which beset him during each session. Only the analysis of this attitude, which also brought out the shame over unconscious passive homosexual tendencies, got us over the impasse.

It is at times of great importance for the general understanding of the case as well as for the immediate interpretative task which one of the two anxiety forms one has to deal with, or whether the one is concealing the other.

But also the conscious therapeutic attitudes and, of course, the unconscious (counter-) transferences, of the therapist vis-à-vis the two types of personalities will prove of great significance in the successful therapeutic handling of either.

E.g., an attitude of kind permissiveness toward a guilt-ridden person may first increase his guilt anxiety manifold—a hostile attitude toward a giving and forgiving parental figure is, of course, much harder to bear than one toward an object that offers some justification in reality. But the consistent maintenance of this attitude will eventually provide the guilt-ridden with the necessary stratum for his "corrective emotional experience," one of confronting his sadistic superego with the presenting kind parent figure.

The same therapeutic attitude might be completely meaningless to a person with a predominant problem of shame, or will be consistently misinterpreted by him. The above-described little episode might serve as an example. The shame-driven patient's unconscious experienced my gesture of trust and encouragement as an additional humiliation which widened the gulf between his (imagined) inferiority and my (projected) superiority.

Similarly the therapeutic effort to get a patient "to experience and express his hostilities" might be decisive in certain cases of guilt-repressed aggressiveness. But to concentrate on the hostilities of the shame-driven will miss the point of his main problem. It might play in with his defense of overcompensation, or it might help to conceal the shame behind the guilt.

It seems to me, however, that there *is* a prerequisite in the analyst's emotional attitude toward the shame-driven without which a successful therapy will be doubtful. I mean the ability of the therapist to identify with, or at least to relate himself to the patient's ego potentialities. It is, of course, at times extremely difficult to even detect the patient's potentialities behind his dense smoke-screens of either self-depreciation or its opposite, four-flushing and braggadocio. But if the therapist cannot sense or find these potentialities rather early in his work with the patient, and if the therapist's ego is not such that he can attain a modicum of genuine *respect* for what potentialities he perceives in this particular patient, then I doubt that this analysis can ever be successful. It is only in such an atmosphere of respect without narcissistic expectations or ambitions that a shame-driven patient can learn to divorce himself from his over-exacting ego ideals.

A lack of sensitivity on the part of the therapist to the degrees of *intensity* of either guilt or shame problems might make for certain untoward transference responses, again with particular characteristics for either kind. A too fast and too energetic breaking down of defenses against the feeling of guilt might lead the patient into a strongly sado-masochistic relationship with the therapist. A similar procedure with a shame-driven individual might leave the latter no escape but to endow the great revealer with omnipotence and save his pride by the knowledge that he is now at least submitting to a God. An unnecessarily protracted course of therapy will be the result in either case.

There is a seeming paradox in the *therapeutic responsiveness* of *shame and guilt.* Whereas it seems evident that shame has definite "progressive" and "self-curative" elements in it, it does not follow at all that a pathological condition with the nuclear problem of shame will yield to therapy easier than one of guilt. Rather the opposite is true. In guilt problems like those underlying certain masochistic syndromes, one can, under favorable conditions, make a remarkable therapeutic advance if one has been merely able to demonstrate to the patient that certain misfortunes are not just happening to him but that he himself has managed to bring them about. That is not so easy with problems of shame. The first therapeutic steps very frequently bring about increased shame and/or increased compensatory activity. The reason for that may lie not only in structural elements of the two emotions, but also in our present cultural atmosphere. Our culture strongly emphasizes comparing and competing—causative of shame tension, and on the other hand, puts a premium on compensatory activity. This makes extremely difficult the therapeutic task of delimiting adaptive techniques from neurotic acting out.

CULTURAL PROBLEMS

B o t h shame and guilt are highly important mechanisms to insure socialization of the individual. Guilt transfers the demands of society through the early primitive parental images. Social conformity achieved through guilt will be essentially one of *submission*. Shame can be brought to the individual more readily in the process of comparing and competing with the peers (siblings, schoolmates, gang, professional group, social class, etc.). Social conformity achieved through shame will be essentially one of *identification*.

One might, therefore, easily expect to find various cultures characterized and differentiated according to the prevalent use of either shame or guilt inducing sanctions to insure social integration. In part II, Milton B. Singer will discuss the validity of current anthropological concepts relative to these problems.

Our own Western culture seems to be undergoing

a gradual change. The highly patriarchal, feudal, and hierarchical society before the Reformation put a high emphasis on guilt. Guilt before God was an accepted and practically unalterable fact; everyone was essentially equal in this, so that there was no distinction nor possibility to achieve any distinction except by degrees of submission; humiliation before God-Father was of the essence of human existence and no matter of shame.

With the Reformation this development reaches a climax. At the same time a new trend emerges. The emphasis on self-responsibility (Luther's *Freiheit eines Christenmenschen*), the importance put on an immanent conscience over and above the allegiance to a transcendental godhead reflects the high degree of "internalization" of guilt.

On the other hand, it contains elements which mark a turning point away from the irrationality of this guilt concept. Although retaining the dogma of the original sin, Protestantism, particularly Calvinism with its division into the "chosen" and the "rejected," opens the door for differentiation and comparison; the emphasis on rationality, work, and success calls for aggressiveness without guilt. Capitalism and technology have further emphasized this trend. Work, previously regarded and experienced as God-inflicted punishment, as drudgery to expiate the pressing sense of guilt, now becomes idealized, a road to accomplishment and distinction. The beggar in early Christianity could be God's child, a successful penitent and even glorified as saint; in Protestant acquisitive status society, he "ought to be ashamed."

It seems that for hundreds of years, social reformers have been vaguely aware of the shortcomings and pitfalls of the social techniques of shame and guilt. Many a Utopian writer has tried to project a society which is cohesive without fear of guilt-creating punishment and without shame-producing competition. No attempt at realization has succeeded so far. Whether such a society is "humanly" possible remains one of the most intriguing riddles of mankind.

Shame Cultures and

Guilt Cultures

CHAPTER

One

INTRODUCTION

IN THE comparative study of cultures it has become practically axiomatic to classify them into shame cultures and guilt cultures.[1] In this classification the shame cultures are many and the guilt cultures are few. "Primitive cultures," with a few exceptions, and practically all the cultures of Asia are regarded as shame cultures which rely principally on shame as an external sanction for assuring conformity to the cultural norms. The reliance on a sense of guilt or "conscience" as an internal sanction is, on the other hand, said to be restricted to the cultures of Western Europe and America. It is also usual to link this classification of shame and guilt cultures to far-reaching interpretations of the economic, social, and moral properties of the cultures.

The guilt cultures—especially those in which the sense of guilt has become highly individualized—are said to be those capable of progressive change, particularly of industrialization, possessed of absolute moral standards which are effectively enforced by a religious "conscience," and dedicated to the welfare and dignity of the individual. The shame cultures contrastingly are said to be static, industrially backward, without absolute moral standards, and dominated by "crowd psychology." In this contrast of cultures Max Weber's thesis that "the Protestant Ethic" was a significant factor in the development of Western European industrial capitalism is transformed into a general formula for modernizing "backward areas": namely, that these "backward" cultures cannot industrialize unless they develop a value system similar to "the Protestant Ethic" and "Protestant personalities" who are driven by a sense of guilt. Where industrialization has relatively recently occurred, as in the Soviet Union, the observation has been made that the required "Protestant personality type" has already appeared, at least as a cultural ideal.[2]

There is in these correlations a consistency which echoes the apologetics of "the white man's burden"; and Kroeber is sufficiently skeptical about it to suggest that "the reputedly independent and separate verdicts of Anglo-Saxon anthropologists on Asiatic, Oceanic, native American, and African cultures, that shame is a far more influential motivation in them than a sense of sin, does not really specifically characterize these cultures nearly so much as its opposite—conscious sinfulness—characterizes Anglo-Saxon and Protestant culture."[3] I also suspect that the aim of these anthropologists—at least in the 1920s and early 1930s—to disprove the universality of the Oedipus complex had something to do with the rare finding of guilt in other cultures.

It is in any case quite easy, once we begin to question the theory of shame and guilt cultures, to point to many developments of modern history which cast serious doubt on the neat correlations between shame and guilt mechanisms on the one hand, and the major trends of technical, social, and moral development on the other. The last two world wars have been waged by and among the most technically advanced "guilt" cultures, not the shame cultures. Many progressive changes have occurred and are going on now without the prior or even simultaneous development of the "Protestant personality": the industrialization of Japan and the more recent beginnings of the process in India and China. There are nonindustrialized cultures, like that of Islam, with absolute moral standards, which are effectively enforced for the general population not by an "inner voice" but by the pressures of law and public opinion. Within the West itself, the belief in the individualized sense of guilt as the standard bearer of civilization and progress has been considerably shaken by studies which seek to link the major pathologies of modern civilization—war, dictatorship, and mental disease—to the "heightened sense of guilt." And some students of the West have discerned the emergence of a new radar-like mechanism of character formation which functions more like the group-mindedness of primitive cultures than like the individualized conscience upon which the industrialized West has prided itself.[4]

I do not believe that it is possible to reconcile these doubts with the theory of shame and guilt cultures in its present form, and I propose in this paper to make some suggestions for reformulation of the theory especially as concerns three major problems: (1) By what general criteria may we distinguish a shame culture from a guilt culture? (2) What kind of psychological data will furnish evidence for the prevalence of shame or guilt in a culture? (3) To what extent may we interpret characteristic anxieties and emotional emphases of a culture as "projections" of unconscious guilt? While I shall be dealing with these problems as they are raised in some of the anthropological literature, the origin and direction of my inquiry owes much to Dr. Piers' illuminating analysis of shame and guilt within the individual.

Two

INTERNAL VERSUS
EXTERNAL SANCTIONS

T H E prevailing criterion for distinguishing shame and guilt cultures has been the distinction between external and internal sanctions. If a culture depends primarily on external sanctions, it is considered to be a shame culture; whereas if it depends on internal sanctions it is a guilt culture. This does not necessarily imply that shame is the only form of external sanction, or guilt the only form of internal sanction, but the assumption is made that shame and guilt are the principal representatives of external and internal sanctions respectively.

An early and influential development of this approach will be found in Margaret Mead's *Cooperation and Competition among Primitive Peoples*. This is a series of individual studies of thirteen primitive cultures, a landmark in the comparative method of testing generalizations about human nature by cross-cultural comparison of similar material. While the major interest of the study is in cooperation and competition, a good deal of attention is also devoted to the formation of character by cultural agencies, and it is in this context that the systematic survey of internal and external sanctions occurs.[5]

Mead defines *sanctions* as "mechanisms by which conformity is obtained, by which desired behavior is induced and undesired behavior prevented." (P. 493) If the individual child "so internalizes the standards that he obeys them in the absence of force exerted from the outside," then he is obeying *internal sanctions*. And "once these are established within the character of the individual they operate automatically." As examples of the operation of internal sanctions, Mead cites obeying a taboo for fear of death or disease, or abstaining from illicit sex activities for fear of punishment by the ghosts.

If, an the other hand, the growing individual has not so internalized his culture's standards, but responds only to "forces which must be set in motion by others"— such as ridicule, abuse, execution of a royal decree—then he is responding to *external sanctions*.

The major internal sanctions found among the thirteen primitive cultures are guilt, anxiety over loss of love, anxiety over loss of health, fear of loss of strength, fear of being shamed, fear of loss of status, anxiety over failure to achieve, pride, fear of offending against the system, and the sense of one's own position, which must be kept inviolate.

The major external sanctions are withdrawal of

health and affection by members of the group, sorcery and accusation of sorcery, threat of starvation, threat of death, punishment of person, destruction of offender's property, expulsion, threat of force, public shaming, divesting of reputation, ritual scolding and ridicule, a well enforced judicial system, and the public invocation of some of the internal sanctions of guilt and pride.

These lists of internal and external sanctions are not, however, a sufficient clue to the classification of the thirteen cultures as shame or guilt cultures. Only two of the thirteen—the Manus and the Arapesh—are classified as guilt cultures, with character structures roughly similar to the Western European. The use of shame as a principal external sanction is said to be characteristic of all of the North American Indian cultures. The remaining cultures using combinations of internal and external sanctions— and occasionally the power of central authority—are not explicitly classified as either shame or guilt cultures.

In Mead's tabulated lists of sanctions, shame appears as an internal sanction in the form of "fear of being shamed," as well as an external sanction in the form of shaming, ridicule, etc. Why then is not shame considered to be as much of an internal sanction as guilt? To this question Mead gives two answers: (1) shame may become an internal sanction when it is strongly developed; and (2) shame requires an audience who know about the misdeed, whereas guilt operates in the psyche without an audience. "In societies in which the individual is controlled by fear of being shamed, he is safe if no one knows of his misdeeds; he can dismiss his misbehavior from his mind . . . but the individual who feels guilt must repent and *atone* for his *sin*." (P. 494) "Guilt is a response to a past threat . . . which seems to be internalized in the character, and re-enactment of analogous situations throughout life invokes the earlier fears and makes it necessary to establish the internal balance of the personality." (P. 494).

This obviously complicates the difference between internal and external sanctions as a criterion for distinguishing shame and guilt cultures, since it adds to that criterion three others: the strength of development of the shame sanctions, the presence or absence of an audience, and the age at which the sanction is internalized. But these qualifications will not suffice to distinguish shame from guilt sanctions. In the tabulated sanctions for the different cultures, shame as an internal sanction appears whenever shaming as an external sanction is listed. So in about seven of these cultures, shame is strongly enough developed to have become an internal sanction. Where it has become an internal sanction, cannot fear of being shamed operate as a sanction even in the absence of an audience? Can it be so easily dismissed from the mind if no audience is physically present? In another paper Mead notes that shame has sometimes been "internalized to such an extent that an Indian alone in the middle of a lake could be so shamed by his paddle breaking that he would commit suicide." [6] Does this not suggest that feelings of shame may be aroused in the absence of an audience?

Perhaps shame does not require that an audience be present physically, but only in fantasy; perhaps the Indian canoeist thought of what people would say when he got back. This is, of course, a common experience: in prospective and retrospective fantasies we anticipate or remember humiliating experiences and feel ashamed. George Bernard Shaw tells in his autobiography of having felt so humiliated by an incident in his childhood that he was not able to master his shame over it and tell anyone about it until he was an old man. But this is not confined to shame, for in feelings of remorse and in apprehensions of discovery and punishment we also experience a kind of guilt which requires a reference to an audience. Even Kant's categorical imperative contains a reference to the audience of all rational men. It is not the presence of an audience (actual or imaginary) which is decisive for distinguishing shame from guilt. Both shame and guilt may be experienced in the actual presence of an audience or when the audience is present only as an internalized "other" (H. S. Sullivan's "eidetic other," G. H. Mead's "me" and "generalized other"). Robinson Crusoe was as much dominated by inner shame as he was by guilt.

That there are forms of guilt dependent on an audience and in this respect resembling the fear of being shamed may be granted, but it may be argued that this does not yet take account of genuine guilt feelings—the unconscious sense of guilt—which is experienced in solitude and contains no conscious or realistic reference to an audience, punishment, or misdeeds. Is this not perhaps the decisive point of difference from shame? The unconscious sense of guilt which produces a restless anxiety pressing for punishment of the individual without any realistic basis has, I suppose, been often enough observed by psychoanalysts to be taken for a fact. Their theory, too, that this sense of guilt derives from hostile feelings acquired in childhood towards punitive parents seems plausible enough. In this meaning, guilt is an internalized response to a past threat—as Margaret Mead calls it. But I do not think that guilt differs from shame even in this respect, for as Piers so well points out, there is also an unconscious form of shame. This form of inner shame may also be without any conscious reference to an audience, and need involve only the anxiety of failing to live up to one's ideals. It, too, may be regarded as an internalized response to a past threat, but what has been internalized are the ideals of the loving parents and the past threat unconsciously reactivated is abandonment by those loving parents and loss of their love.

The practical conclusion of this discussion is that we cannot distinguish shame and guilt in terms of external and internal sanctions respectively, for there are "inner" forms of shame paralleling almost exactly the forms of guilt. Nor can we save the internal-external criterion by saying that shame requires an audience and guilt does not, or that guilt involves a re-enactment of a childhood response and shame does not, for these additional criteria will only serve to differentiate among the forms of shame and among the forms of guilt but not to distinguish shame from guilt. Excessive reliance on the internal-external criterion for distinguishing shame from guilt, and the failure to develop more adequate criteria, has in the past been responsible for a number of confusions in the attempts to use shame and guilt sanctions as a basis for classifying cultures. Some of the most common of these are the identification of inner shame with guilt; the failure to see that "internal" sanctions like fear of loss of status and position, and anxiety over failure to achieve, and over loss of love and pride, are very closely related to shame sanctions (recognizing this might change the classification of Manus and Arapesh from guilt to shame cultures); the confusion of conscious and unconscious guilt; and the practically universal assumption that the presence of "shaming," ridicule, and other forms of insult imply a shame culture, despite the fact that such "external" sanctions might generate guilt and are not in any case necessary for arousing shame. These confusions have combined to encourage the emphasis on the external side of shame and on the internal side of guilt, an emphasis congenial to the notion that most cultures of the world use shame as an external sanction and have yet not advanced to the internal moral sanctions characteristic of our own culture. There is little question that the classification of cultures into shame and guilt cultures would have to be substantially changed once we abandoned the internal-external sanction criterion. We might lose a neat classification but we should gain much greater understanding of the role of shame and guilt in different cultures.

We must therefore seek new criteria to distinguish shame from guilt if we are to use these psychological states to characterize cultures. Within the individual, it is possible to differentiate unconscious shame from unconscious guilt as Dr. Piers does. He distinguishes them in terms of a difference in the kind of internalized norm violated and the kind of unconscious threat activated: unconscious guilt is aroused by impulses to transgress the internalized prohibitions of punishing parents, and the unconscious threat is mutilation; unconscious shame, on the other hand, is aroused by a failure to live up to the internalized ideals of loving parents, and the unconscious threat is abandonment. To what extent these criteria can be applied to psychometric and cultural data, and whether all conscious forms of shame and guilt can be reduced to unconscious anxieties, are questions that will concern us in the next two chapters.

Three

PSYCHOMETRIC DATA ON SHAME AND GUILT IN AMERICAN INDIAN CULTURES

T H E   E V I D E N C E on which the classification of cultures as shame or guilt cultures has been based has for the most part been drawn from the observations of anthropologists and from the reports and interpretations of native informants. More recently the development of psychometric tests and questionnaires has prompted some anthropologists and psychologists to use standardized psychological data for classifying cultures. There are many problems raised by this development—can such tests be standardized cross-culturally and will they replace the more traditional methods of cultural and social observation? It is much too early to make dogmatic pronouncements on these issues; but the fact that anthropologists look upon these psychological tests as a possibly useful adjunct to their methods, while the psychologists regard them as exact and quantitative substitutes for the pre-scientific "impressionistic" methods, seems to point to a fundamental difference of opinion as to what constitutes reliable evidence in comparative cultural studies and by what methods it may be gathered.

Although standardized psychological data are becoming more and more a regular feature of anthropological monographs, there are as yet few full scale comparative studies which make use of such data. One of the pioneer studies which has data about shame and guilt is the Indian Education Project sponsored jointly by the University of Chicago Committee on Human Development and the Office of Indian Affairs.[7] This is a cooperative and interdisciplinary study of five American Indian Tribes—Hopi, Navaho, Papago, Sioux, and Zuni—and of a midwestern community. For each of the tribes and for the midwestern community there are descriptions of the culture and of the individual life cycles, data from standardized psychological tests given to representative samples of children six to eighteen, and selected personality profiles. In this chapter I shall consider whether the test data support the conclusion that American Indian cultures are predominantly shame cultures, especially as compared to Western guilt culture, of which the midwestern community is a representative.

In their monograph on the Navaho, Kluckhohn and Leighton present what appears to be clear-cut evidence in one of these tests—Stewart's Emotional Response Test —for the shame-guilt theory. In this test the children are asked to describe occasions when they felt shame, anger, happiness, sadness, fear, and the best and worst things that could happen to them. For purpose of comparison, the responses under each emotion were classified into separate categories and counted. Tables were then constructed showing the percentage of responses concerning each emotion made by the children tested in each tribe. By inspecting a table containing these percentages for all tribes and the midwestern group, we can tell at a glance something about the comparative incidence of the various emotions and their objects, at least at the conscious level. Those results are then compared with the results of the projective tests (Rorschach and T.A.T.) to see whether the patterns of feelings at the "unconscious" level agree with the conscious patterns.

The responses to the questions about occasions when the children felt shame were classified into the following categories:

1. Making a poor appearance in public.
2. Embarrassment in presence of others.
3. Poverty and neglect in home.
4. Loss or damage to property.
5. Personal failure and inadequacy.
6. Bad behavior with peers of opposite sex.
7. Personal bad behavior and aggressiveness.
8. Rowdiness of companions.
9. Bad behavior of others towards others.
10. Discipline.
11. Aggression by others.
12. Embarrassment of groups to which subject belongs.
13. Miscellaneous.

It is the responses to the questions about shame that according to Kluckhohn and Leighton contain the crucial evidence. These responses are presented in the following table:

Responses of Navaho and white children
concerning shame;
percentage distribution by source of shame.[8]

SOURCE OF SHAME	PERCENTAGE OF RESPONSES	
	Navaho	White
Self-consciousness	43	12
Making poor personal appearance	22	10
Embarrassment before others	21	2
Guilt	16	49
Failure or inadequacy	11	21
Bad behavior and aggressiveness	5	28
Other scattered responses	41	39

On the basis of this data and of their intimate knowledge of the Navaho, Kluckhohn and Leighton draw the familiar conclusions that the white children are motivated by the "internal" sanctions of conscience, whereas the Navaho children are motivated more by the "external" sanction of public opinion:

On the basis of these findings one might expect a white child to feel uncomfortable and "guilty" after stealing an orange whether anyone found out about it or not, whereas a Navaho child would be more likely to enjoy the orange without feeling guilt, but would be "self-conscious" if someone caught him.[9]

The explanation which Kluckhohn and Leighton give for the apparent absence of internal sanctions in the Navaho children is that:

> they have not internalized the standards of their parents and other elders but, rather, accept these standards as part of the external environment to which an adjustment must be made . . . "divine discontent" is an emotion foreign to the normal Navaho.[10]

In other words, the Navaho are not "socialized" in the sense of having derived ego-ideals or superegos from their parents and social environment. They are "socialized" only in the sense of being responsive to the demands of their environment. Why they should be so responsive to these demands is not entirely clear from this account. One reason presumably is the fear of punishment and another is the sheer intimacy of social life:

> "Shame" naturally develops as a major sanction in societies where almost identical fears are shaped and in which there is so little privacy and such constant face-to-face relationships among the people who really count in each other's lives that small peccadillos cannot be hidden. In the circumstances of Navaho life a pose of omnipotence or omniscience on the part of parents would be speedily and almost daily exposed.[11]

Kluckhohn and Leighton also seem to endorse the theory that it is the reliance on external shame that makes Navaho society "static" and the reliance on internal guilt that makes white society "progressive."

It is believed by some that "progress" occurs in societies of the Christian tradition largely because each socialized individual is trying to avoid the self-reproach that would be incurred by failing to live up to the ideals inculcated in childhood. Navaho society is (or would be if not under continual pressure from white society) much more static, since "shame" ("I would feel very uncomfortable if anyone saw me deviating from accepted norms") plays the psychological role which "conscience" or "guilt" ("I am unworthy for I am not living up to the high standards represented by my parents") has in the Christian tradition.[12]

All these are familiar conclusions, and are applied by other writers not only to a comparison of a Navaho and a midwestern community, but to a comparison of Western and non-western cultures in general. Depending on their degree of sympathy for non-western cultures and their degree of antipathy to Western culture, these writers look upon the members of non-western cultures either as incompletely "socialized" and lacking the moral mainsprings of progress, or as having adopted an alternative mechanism of socialization which, it is usually intimated, achieves more in the way of social cohesion and individual happiness than the Western obsession with the sense of sin.[13]

This sharp contrast between the Navaho and white children is not sustained by the data from the other Indian groups. The Navaho pattern of shame responses is not characteristic of all the Indian children. The Hopi and the Sioux, on the contrary, rank as high as the midwestern group in their mention of "personal bad behavior and aggressiveness" as a source of shame, and such mentions are to be taken as evidence of a sense of guilt according to Kluckhohn and Leighton. This difference in the absence of guilt feelings between the Navaho and some of the other Indian groups is also indicated by the T.A.T. and Rorschach tests.[14] There does not seem to be a uniform pattern of shame and guilt characterizing the Indian groups, but a range of variation among them that makes any sharp dichotomy between them and the white group misleading.

This caution is further urged upon us by the results of some of the other psychological tests—particularly the "Moral Ideology" test and the test for "immanent justice" and "animism"—and by a survey of some of the most frequent "values" or "themes" turning up in all the tests.

In the "Moral Ideology" test, the children are asked to list what boys and girls of their age think are good and bad things to do, and who would praise or blame if such things were done. This test aims to discover the "official" as distinct from the "private" ideology, that is, the moral values and beliefs which are commonly held by members of the group. It is assumed that the "moral ideology" influences behavior, but it is not assumed that actual behavior will correspond to the test responses: "a person may do things he says are bad to do, and fail to do things he says are good to do." [15] The one major result of this test is that all the Indian groups are aware of moral judgments, that is, the children distinguish easily between good and bad actions, and know who would praise or blame respectively. Beyond this, the results are complex: each group reveals a fairly consistent pattern of moral values, but there is much variation among them, and the meaning of the results for a particular group is sometimes quite opaque. It is particularly difficult to reconcile this test data with the generalization that the Indian cultures are shame rather than guilt cultures. The Indian children, e.g., mention much more frequently than the white children "aggression" and "evil thoughts" as "bad things"; ordinarily we should take that as evidence of guilt rather than shame. It is usually assumed that shame is connected with a sensitivity to the praise and blame of agemates and "everybody," whereas guilt is supposed to be connected with parental discipline and eventually self-discipline. Yet the Indian children (except the Hopi and Sioux) mention "agemates" and "everybody" less frequently than the white children, and "parents" more frequently. This is particularly striking in the case of the Zuni children, who seem to be very much aware of strong parental discipline, although theirs is supposed to be a shame culture. "Self" and "Deity" are both mentioned less frequently by the Indian children than by the white, as "praisers" and "blamers," whereas "the recipient of the act" is mentioned more frequently. From this type of data we can only conclude that the patterns of shame and guilt among these Indian cultures are quite varied and complex, and that their awareness of moral standards and sanctions does not differ essentially from that found in Western culture.

Further evidence for the basic similarity of the Indian value systems with that of the white is provided by the fact that such values as hard work, desire for property and possessions, self-denial of personal pleasures, and a strict sexual morality rank as high in three of the Indian cultures (including the Navaho) as they do in the midwestern community. Since these particular values are generally regarded as major elements of the "Protestant Ethic," programs to modernize primitive cultures by teaching them these values may be carrying coals to Newcastle. It is of course true that two other values of the "Protestant" constellation—desire for personal achievement and the sense of individual moral responsibility—are not very prominent among the Indian value systems.

The midwestern children definitely show a greater expressed concern about personal achievement and about personal failure than most of the Indian children. However, the responsiveness of Indian children to praise of individual achievement in private,[16] and the widespread use in primitive groups of praise and other rewards as an incentive for children to learn their social tasks,[17] shows that the "maturation drive" is not absent among these groups. Primitive cultures probably do not permit this drive to become so closely linked to ideals of personal growth and self-realization as it is in our culture (where, of course, it is also geared to culturally defined imperatives). These cultural and environmental barriers to self-development in primitive cultures have a lot to do, I suspect, with generating a chronic "shyness shame."

Evidence for the concept of individual moral responsibility is more difficult to collect and appraise because this category was not explicitly used in the tests and because it is in any case highly ambiguous. We may mean by the concept of moral responsibility the complex of ideas and beliefs which includes awareness of a distinction between good and bad actions, a belief that good actions are rewarded and bad ones punished, and a feeling of shame or guilt when a bad action is contemplated or carried through. In this sense all the Indian groups have a very distinct concept of moral responsibility.[18] They believe in non-human agencies which judge and punish human actions, and include among these not only ancestral ghosts and supernatural beings but also ordinary animals and objects. These ideas have been called the belief in immanent justice and in animism. To test for them Havighurst and his associates told the children the following story:

> This is a story about two boys. These two boys, named Jack and Paul, were out walking and they came to a melon field. Each of them stole a melon and ran off with it. But the owner of the field saw them and ran after them. He caught Jack and punished him, but Paul got away. The same afternoon, Paul was chopping some wood, and the axe slipped and cut his foot.

The children were then asked three questions about the story:

1. Why do you think Paul's foot was cut?
2. If Paul did not steal the melon, would he cut his foot?
3. Did the axe know that he stole the melon?

Using the answers to the first two questions as a basis for ascertaining a belief in *immanent justice* and answers to the third question for determining the degree of belief in *animism*, Havighurst found that practically all the Indian children showed a very strong belief in immanent justice and animism. Moreover, he found that the belief in immanent justice did not decrease with age, as Piaget and other investigators have found with white children, but actually increased. In the case of animistic beliefs, there was a slight decrease with age.[19] This would seem to show that such beliefs are an essential feature of the primitive world view.

These beliefs in animism and in immanent justice actually influence the thought and behavior of the Indian children and certainly resemble the more specialized Western conceptions of supernatural moral guidance and retribution. The Papago study describes these beliefs as functioning like "a vaguely defined religious conscience" (p. 210), and the Hopi study as "a conscience of group-bound responsibility on the religious level." (P. 107).

When we ask whether this moral or religious conscience is "individualized and internalized" among the Indians as it is alleged to be among us, ambiguities arise. In the sense that the Indian children feel a personal responsibility for judging, rewarding, and punishment good and bad actions and for leading a "good life," the Indians certainly have an individualized conscience. But they do not generally limit an individual's moral responsibility to the judgment and punishment of his own actions. In this sense it is probably true to say that they do not emphasize the conception of individual moral responsibility as much as we do. But the point of this contrast should not be that the individual among them lacks a sense of being responsible for his actions; it is rather that they do not limit moral responsibility to this alone, that while the individual feels responsible for his own actions he also feels responsible for the actions of others, and in fact feels morally implicated in practically everything that happens to his group and in the universe.[20]

The comparative psychometric data gathered by the Indian Education Study do not support the generalization that American Indian cultures are predominantly "shame cultures" which lack the internal sanctions of guilt and moral conscience. On the contrary these data can be read to support the conclusions that among some of these Indian cultures the sense of guilt plays an important role—both as a personal emotion and in the official moral code; that their value systems have much in common with those Western value systems which are considered to be dominated by a sense of guilt; that while they do not stress a value like personal achievement, the Indian children are not unresponsive to it; and that a moral and religious conscience with the associated concepts of moral punishment and reward is a characteristic feature of all of them. The only respects in which the value system of the midwestern community seems to differ from the Indian systems of value is that it tends to limit the sense of moral responsibility to the individual's own actions, and to esteem personal achievement as a culturally approved ideal.

But we must not put too much weight on evidence of this type. Psychometric methods are new, and their application to comparative cultural studies is highly experimental. The well known difficulties in measuring attitudes, beliefs, emotion, and values are greatly multiplied when the measurements have to be standardized for different cultures. It may be well, in closing this topic, to mention some of these difficulties:

1) First there is the problem of language. The Zuni, e.g., have but one word for "shame," and the tester may have considerable difficulty in finding out what relation this has to the various kinds of shame we distinguish and to our concept of guilt.[21]

2) Next is the fact that different cultures may actually "condition" feelings of shame and guilt differently, so that the tester's criteria for interpreting shame and guilt responses may lead him astray because they may reflect the criteria of a particular culture. Is it not using a culturally limited criterion to assume that tendencies to personal aggression equally arouse guilt feelings in all cultures?

3) Even within a single culture different investigators may have different criteria for shame and guilt: Kluckhohn and Leighton, e.g., classify personal failure and inadequacy as a source of guilt, but according to Piers' criterion it is a source of shame feelings.

4) Intimate knowledge of a group's moral code and

of the manner and quality of enforcement procedure are also essential for a proper interpretation of the test responses. If a particular type of action is mentioned less frequently as a source of shame in culture A than in culture B, this might mean that it arouses less shame in A than in B, or it might mean that it arouses so much shame in A that it will not even be mentioned.

5) It is usual to assume that these various cultural and conventional influences on psychological tests can be circumvented by the use of projective tests which get at the "real," "underlying," and "unconscious" emotions and attitudes. But projective tests, like other tests, have to be presented through linguistic media and in specific cultural settings, and their results are definitely influenced by the peculiarities of cultural content.[22] And even when these cultural influences can be discerned and discounted, there is at present no way whereby the projective tests themselves can clearly separate conscious from unconscious processes.[23]

6) Finally, there is the circumstance that the various psychometric tests and questionnaires are frequently not independent of one another or of cultural methods, so that the validity of any particular test cannot be established by showing that its results agree with those of other tests or with anthropological observations.

Which of these difficulties are inherent in cross-cultural testing and which will be overcome with improved technique is a question for the future to decide.

Four

PSYCHOANALYTIC VERSUS CULTURAL INTERPRETATIONS OF GUILT CULTURES

I N T H E studies we have so far discussed, the assumption that "guilt cultures" are very exceptional and rare and that "shame cultures" are the rule is taken for granted. There are, however, some studies in which evidence is presented to support just the opposite theory—that the sense of guilt is to be found in most if not all cultures. Some of the very same Indian cultures—the Hopi, Navaho, Ojibwa—which in the previous studies were described as dominated by external shame sanctions are now described as being pervaded by guilt.[24] The evidence for this ubiquitous sense of guilt is found in the fears, anxieties, tensions, and hostilities of group life, whatever the form in which these fears and anxieties are expressed: myths, gossip, sorcery and magic, drinking, anxiety about disease and the food supply are all grist for the guilt mill.

This evidence is generally not direct, but depends on a framework of theoretical interpretation which links the emotional emphases of a culture to the sense of guilt. There are in the main two kinds of theoretical systems of interpretation now in use—the psychoanalytic and the cultural. The psychoanalytic type of interpretation ultimately derives an unconscious sense of guilt from oedipal conflicts or at least from repressed hostilities. Because everyone is supposed to have repressed hostile impulses toward his parents, about which he feels guilt, everyone will "project," "displace," and "rationalize" these impulses into cultural channels. Therefore if we find specific forms of anxiety and hostility in any aspect of the culture we are, according to this theory, to interpret them as an expression of unconscious guilt even if the "manifest" and conscious explanation of the anxiety given by members of the culture seems to have nothing to do with the "family romance."

The cultural type of interpretation takes the "manifest" and conscious explanations of anxiety more seriously. If, e.g., the Saulteaux Indians invest certain disease situations with "disproportionate" anxiety, this is not merely, writes Hallowell, the projected neurotic anxiety of unconscious guilt but must also be understood in relation to the Saulteaux theories of disease and their belief that illness is a penalty for infractions of the moral code. The value attached to health and a long life and the fear that one may be punished for "bad conduct" through illness are thus important cultural factors in explaining the anxiety. What transforms the anxiety into guilt anxiety is not the unconscious oedipal conflict but a very conscious reference to the moral code and world view of the culture.

The distance between these two types of interpretation is not actually so great as my bald statement of them suggests. The mutual influences of psychoanalysis and cultural anthropology have created a variety of intermediate theoretical positions which form a practically continuous bridge from the Freudian to the cultural side. It is of course well known that the type of interpretation employed by Freud himself in *Totem and Taboo, Civilization and Its Discontents,* and *Moses and Monotheism* has never been accepted by social scientists because of its effort to explain social processes in terms of individual psychology and its stress on the biological inheritance of acquired characters. However, once they recovered from the outrage at having the origin of all human culture, as well as of particular cultures explained in terms of a phylogenetically determined Oedipus complex, anthropologists responded more constructively to psychoanalysis.[25] Unqualified resistance was replaced by partial assimilation of a modified doctrine. Róheim, one of the first anthropologists to apply psychoanalysis, modified Freud's phylogenetic theories, but he retained an ontogenetic theory of character formation which assumed that the Oedipus complex, and therefore a sense of guilt, was universal, because infantile traumata and a prolonged and helpless infancy were universal, although variations in early childhood experience could also produce variations in group character.[26] Malinowski—and more recently Kardiner—carried this modification one step farther by arguing that there was not just one kind of Oedipus complex but as many different kinds of psychological "complexes" as there are varieties of culturally standardized child-rearing patterns in the world. And a culture may even be without any kind of oedipal conflicts or a sense of guilt if it lacks a particular kind of child-rearing pattern.[27]

The Kardiner approach correlates the occurrence of guilt in a culture with the special child-rearing pattern: parental punishment for disobedience and love for obedience. This pattern is the one found in Western culture and produces the characteristic Oedipus complex and sense of guilt which Freud described. But it is the thesis of these studies that this is not a universal pattern, that other child-rearing patterns are found in other cultures where the typical Oedipus complex and a sense of guilt do not appear. Of the primitive cultures studied by the Kardiner group, only the Tanala of Madagascar are found to have a pattern similar to ours with an Oedipus complex and a sense of guilt. The Comanche, who do not punish children for disobedience and who bestow love and praise for achievement, are said to be free of a sense of guilt and of the concept that misfortune is due to sin, although shame remains a sanction. Where there is neither love given for obedience nor consistent punishment for disobedience, as among the Marquesans and the

Alorese, there is no Western form of conscience, but there is a sense of shame. Kardiner suggests that the sense of shame is a residue found in every culture where the conditions for winning the approval of others do not depend on renouncing the satisfaction of biological needs.[28]

But whether they find guilt or shame, the concentration of these studies on child rearing as the primary cultural variable has led to an underestimation of such other variables as beliefs and values, contact and conflict with other cultures, and the historical development of particular institutions in a particular geographical environment. It is their effort to give due attention to these latter variables that marks off the third type of synthesis between psychoanalysis and anthropology. In the studies of this type—of which Hallowell and the later Mead and Benedict are illustrative—it is assumed that specific beliefs and values may be as important sources of shame and guilt as child-rearing practices and may in fact be as much causes of the child-rearing pattern as its effects. They do not assume that any correspondence between a child-rearing practice and some other institution automatically proves that the former causes the latter, but lean rather to an assumption of circular interaction of diverse cultural variables, including child rearing, within the framework of a casual system or of a total configuration of culture.[29]

This third type of modification of the Freudian interpretation seems to join hands with the non-Freudian kinds of interpretation which emphasize cultural factors.

The effort to test and if possible to disprove Freud by comparative cultural data has thus actually resulted in a substantial assimilation of psychoanalytic concepts and theories by anthropologists. Yet it would be premature to say that the integration is complete and successful. None of the integrations of psychoanalysis and anthropology has succeeded in developing workable criteria for the simultaneous application of psychoanalytic and cultural interpretations to cultural materials. Psychoanalysis has undoubtedly established the operation of such mechanisms as "projection," "displacement," and "rationalization," and has shown their relation to childhood experiences in individual psychological development. But the data for this are drawn from an individual's most intimate emotional and intellectual processes. When an effort is made to psychoanalyze a culture, the evidential data are of a different order and quality. They are rarely based on the psychoanalysis of a sample of individuals but come from ethnographic observation, psychological tests, brief interviews, interpretations of myths and folklore, etc. Inferences from such data to unconscious psychological processes in individuals must remain highly indirect and precarious. If we know that one culture has a characteristic anxiety about disease, is it possible with the criteria now available to establish that this anxiety is wholly or in part a "projection" or "displacement" of unconscious guilt? I do not believe so. Neither the intensity of the anxiety, nor its inappropriateness in relation to the objective facts, nor its having been acquired in childhood would be sufficient criteria for this purpose. For if the anxiety had developed in the culture as a consequence of historical experience with epidemics or as a consequence of a world view which interprets disease as a punishment for misconduct, it might still be intense, objectively inappropriate, and taught to children. In that case we could still relate such anxiety to guilt feelings but these would not be unconscious; they would be conscious guilt feelings which can be explained in terms of the beliefs and values of the culture. In the absence of criteria and evidence which will adequately differentiate conscious and unconscious guilt, psychoanalytic interpretations of cultures and anxieties will compete disadvantageously with historical, social, and cultural interpretations. This can be illustrated by reference to the discussion of the role of the sense of guilt in cultural evolution.

In *Civilization and Its Discontents* Freud has called the heightening of the sense of guilt the most important problem in the evolution of culture. (P. 81) This is an unconscious sense of guilt "not perceived as such . . . and . . . to a large extent unconscious," or coming to expression "as a sort of *malaise*, a dissatisfaction, for which people seek other motivations." (Pp. 82–83) The explanation for this increase in the unconscious sense of guilt he finds in the development of a "cultural superego" which sets up increasingly severe ethical ideals and standards, particularly against aggression. Under the burden of unconscious guilt produced by this civilizing trend and the additional temptation of modern weapons, mankind, he suggests, may be on the verge of neurotic self-destruction.

This psychoanalysis of modern civilization, Freud warns, is only a hypothetical speculation based on an analogy with the development of the unconscious sense of guilt in individuals. Yet the analogy fails in a very crucial respect: in the psychoanalysis of individual anxiety, the analyst controls his inferences of unconscious guilt by the most detailed knowledge of the patient's dreams and emotional associations; in the psychoanalysis of cultures no corresponding data are available. In fact the data to which Freud appeals—both in *Civilization and Its Discontents* and in *Moses and Monotheism*, where he tries to trace the formation of a specific "cultural superego"—are cultural and historical, referring to historical changes in ethical systems and in technology. And do not these same data suggest an alternative interpretation of the evolution of culture which does not require the assumption of an increase in the unconscious sense of guilt?

Such an alternative interpretation may be inferred from Redfield's theories which suggest that the progress of civilization reduces rather than increases the burden of *conscious* guilt.[30] According to Redfield, the precivilized or "primitive" world view is a moral one in the sense that everything that happens is perceived as being related to the violation or maintenance of the group's ethical code. "To primitive man the universe is spun of duty and ethical judgment." An individual whose conscience is dominated by this moral interpretation of the universe will feel morally responsible for every piece of good or bad fortune which happens to the group, but he will also hold all the other members of the group responsible for it. And even individual good or bad fortune will be attributed, not solely to the moral qualities of the recipient, but to the virtues and vices of friends, enemies, witches, and magic helpers as well. The primitive conscience is thus a social conscience in the sense that it shares its guilts and anxieties with others. Different cultures will, of course, differ in the detailed content of the moral code, methods of detecting and punishing violators, degree of specificity in defining crimes, etc., but the general feeling that no single individual is *wholly* to blame or *wholly* blameless for his own or his group's bad fortune seems to be a common feature of all of them.

In the primitive ethos and world view, each individual's moral failures and achievements, his moral transgressions and conformities, are linked to his personal welfare and to the welfare of the group. And conversely, the general welfare of the group and the private welfare of each are dependent on the sum-total moral virtues and vices of the individual members. Drought, disease, bad crops, poor hunting, defeat in war all have moral significance, because they are seen in the beliefs of many primitive cultures as punishment for misbehavior and misconduct. Since these misfortunes are not limited to the "guilty" individual but may affect the entire group, everyone has a stake in enforcing conformity to the ethos; and everyone, until "the" criminal act or person is identified, experiences guilt feelings as he reviews his own record of past deviations from the group code.

With the development of civilization Redfield sees this primitive world view transformed: science and systematic knowledge turn a personified cosmos which "cares" about human affairs into a vast network of impersonal cause and effect, to or for which the individual can hardly feel any moral responsibility; within human society itself responsibility is specialized and delimited by a complex division of labor, full-time specialists, formal legal systems, and voluntary contractual arrangements; and the compelling and unquestioned rightness of the isolated and homogeneous primitive ethos gives way under the impact of increasing numbers, migrations, and communication to conflicts of ethical standards, and conscious efforts at moral criticism and reform.

If this picture of the evolution of civilization is correct, primitive man has a greater burden of guilt than civilized man, for he feels morally related to the entire universe as well as to his group, there are few specialists to whom he can delegate responsibility, and his standards are in general unequivocal and unrelenting in their demands on him. But such comparisons are not easily made precise and quantitative. There are in primitive cultures ritual and magical means for transferring and reducing guilt.[31] Moreover, can we say that the moral responsibility felt for an entire universe that is as limited as most primitive conceptions of the cosmos are, is "greater than" the responsibility felt by a civilized individual for himself, his family, his co-religionists, or his nation? And is not the strain of being exposed to rapidly changing and conflicting moral standards more conducive to guilt than the pressure of a stable and uniform code? Even if the individual in modern civilization does not feel morally responsible for much more than himself, this self may mean so much and its standards aim so high that the load of conscious guilt (and of shame) may weigh very heavily on him.

These difficulties in making precise historical comparisons apply even more strongly to Freud's theory of civilization and so do not give us any reason for preferring that theory to a cultural theory like Redfield's which has a distinct advantage over Freud's in that it infers only "manifest" and conscious meanings from the historical and cultural data, whereas Freud's theory infers in addition "latent" and unconscious meanings. Whether civilization has brought with it an increase or decrease in the burden of guilt is a question we cannot now answer with any practical or scientific certainty, but with the present kinds of available evidence we are not likely to increase the degree of certainty by reducing the question to a problem about an unconscious sense of guilt.

SUMMARY AND CONCLUSIONS

THE MAJOR conclusions of our examination of the theory of shame and guilt cultures may now be summarized as follows:

1) There are sufficient reasons for doubting the prevailing assumption that most cultures of the world are shame cultures, and that Western culture is one of the rare guilt cultures, to warrant a careful reconsideration of the distinction between shame and guilt cultures and of the presumed correlation between guilt cultures and moral and technical progress.

2) Neither the distinction between internal and external sanctions, nor the additional criteria of reference to an audience and internalized past threat, suffice to differentiate shame from guilt. These criteria can be used to mark off the following parallel levels of shame and guilt: (a) feelings of shame or guilt aroused in the physical presence of an audience; (b) feelings of shame or guilt

aroused in the mental presence of an audience, i.e., in the presence of a fantasy or "eidetic" audience; (c) feelings of shame or guilt aroused without conscious or "realistic" reference to an actual or imaginary audience and presumably representing a reactivation of anxieties originally aroused in childhood by parental disapproval or punishment; and (d) feelings of shame and guilt aroused without conscious reference to a physical or fantasy audience and presumably depending only on abstract moral principles accepted by the self.

But on any of these levels, the differentiation between shame and guilt cannot be made on the basis of the above criteria. Piers' conception of shame as the anxiety aroused by failure to live up to internalized parental ideals under the unconscious threat of abandonment and of guilt as the anxiety aroused by transgression of internalized parental prohibitions under the unconscious threat of mutilation, offers a very promising criterion for distinguishing "unconscious" shame from "unconscious" guilt within the individual.

The use of the criterion of internal versus external sanctions has in the past prompted confusion between guilt and internalized shame, between conscious and unconscious guilt, and between external measures of "shaming" and the feelings and fear of shame.

3) The comparative psychometric data of the Indian Education Study do not support the generalization that American Indian cultures rely principally on shame as an external sanction. The data from these psycholog-

ical tests show a good deal of variation with respect to the incidence of shame and guilt among these cultures: they tend to indicate a significant role for guilt among some of them and the presence of moral judgment and a sense of moral responsibility among all of them. There is also evidence in these data for some of the major values of the "Protestant Ethic," although the desire for personal achievement and an individualized moral responsibility which restricts the objects of responsibility to the self are not prominent cultural values.

Comparative psychological data must be used with great caution in cultural studies, since psychometric methods are still in their infancy and their cross-cultural standardization raises many as yet unsolved problems.

4) A tendency of some studies to find more guilt cultures than formerly does not depend on new direct evidence but on inferences drawn with the help of psychoanthropological theories. These theories combine psychoanalytic and cultural interpretation in varying degrees, and not always successfully, because they lack adequate criteria and evidence for identifying "latent" and "unconscious" processes in cultural and social data. In this respect, attempts to psychoanalyze cultures not only do not live up to the standards of evidence and controlled inference maintained in the psychoanalysis of individuals, but they come into direct conflict with historical and cultural explanations of the same "manifest" data. The argument is illustrated by comparing Freud's and a cultural theory of the role of guilt in cultural evolution. This

comparison suggests that the kind of moral and technical progress that is characteristic of the development of civilization in general and Western civilization in particular does not depend, as Freud thought, on repression and an increase in the unconscious sense of guilt, but is associated with the delimitation and specialization of the sense of moral responsibility. It further suggests that this emergence of an individual-centered moral order is itself the product of such civilizing processes as the growth of knowledge and the contact of diverse cultures. So far as the "burden of unconscious guilt" is concerned, there is no evidence to indicate that it is any greater for civilized peoples than it was for pre-civilized peoples.

5) Whether, then, we consider the criterion of internal and external sanctions, or the cross-cultural psychometric data, or the psychoanalytic interpretations of cultures, we cannot find sufficient evidence to justify the theory that most cultures of the world are shame cultures and that they are morally and technically "backward" because they are not dominated by a sense of guilt. What evidence there is, tends to support the conclusion that the sense of guilt *and* the sense of shame are found in most cultures, and that the quantitative distribution of these sanctions has little to do with the "progressive" or "backward" character of a culture.

6) Psychological characterizations and comparisons of cultures—whether they are made in terms of shame and guilt, or in terms of personality types and "national characters"—are of low validity because they seek

to isolate "pure" psychological categories. Their validity and fruitfulness will increase as they abandon this "psychologism" and develop instead characterizing constructs in which the emotional emphases of a culture are integrally related to cultural values, world view, overt behavior, and features of social organization. Max Weber's construction of a "Protestant Ethic" is one example of such a more complex kind of characterization. While it is still of some value for cultural characterization, it has tended, under the influence of excessive psychological interpretations, to become a designation for a generalized sense of guilt or "Protestant personality type," the absence of which is regarded as equivalent to moral and technical backwardness. I believe, on the contrary, that "backward" peoples do have guilt feelings about many things but that they simply do not feel guilty—or ashamed—that they happen to be in a preindustrial stage of civilization. Bringing them into industrial civilization is not a matter of getting them to substitute guilt sanctions for shame sanctions, but rather of their accepting the complex of values, beliefs, and practices which prevail in industrialized societies.

NOTES

Notes to Part I

1. Sigmund Freud, "Drei Abhandlungen zur Sexualtheorie," *Gesammelte Werke* (London: Imago Publishing Co., 1942), 5:50 ff.
2. *Ibid.*, p. 56. Author's translation. A. A. Brill (*The Basic Writings of Sigmund Freud*. New York: Modern Library, 1938, p. 569) translated this passage erroneously: "The force which opposes the desire for looking and through which the latter is eventually abolished is shame."
3. *Ibid.*, p. 78. Author's translation. Curiously enough, A. A. Brill (*Ibid.*, p. 583) left out "fixated by heredity" (*hereditär fixierte*).
4. Charles Darwin, *The Expression of the Emotions in Man and Animal* (London: John Murray, 1872). See particularly chapter 13 on blushing, etc.
5. Herman Nunberg, "Psychoanalyse des Schamgefuehls," *Allgemeine Neurosenlehre auf Psychoanalytischer Grundlage* (Bern: Hans Huber, 1932), reprinted in *Psychoanalytische Bewegung* 4 (1932): 505-7.
6. Otto Fenichel, *The Psychoanalytic Theory of Neurosis* (New York: W. W. Norton & Company, Inc., 1945), p. 69.
7. *Ibid.*, p. 139. See also O. Fenichel, "The Scoptophilic Instinct and Identification," *International Journal of Psycho-Analysis* 18 (1937).
8. Norman Reider, "The Sense of Shame," *Samiksa* 3 (1950): 147.
9. Erik H. Erikson, *Childhood and Society* (New York: W. W. Norton & Company, Inc., 1963), p. 252.
10. Franz Alexander, "Remarks about the Relation of Inferiority Feelings to Guilt Feelings," *International Journal of Psycho-Analysis* 19 (1938): 41. In this paper Alexander outlines the typical defenses against the two forms of inner tension. Against guilt: a) avoidance of expressing hostile tendencies; b) self-punishment; c) provocative behavior; and d) projection. The typical reactions to shame are: a) increased hostile aggression; b) depreciative competition; and c) to fantasy oneself superior.
11. Franz Alexander, *Fundamentals of Psychoanalysis* (New York: W. W. Norton & Company, Inc., 1948).
12. Sigmund Freud, *The Ego and the Id*, trans. Joan Riviere, ed.

James Strachey (New York: W. W. Norton & Company, Inc., 1962), p. 24.

13. Heinz Hartmann, Ernst Kris, and Rudolf M. Loewenstein, "Comments on the Formation of Psychic Structure," *The Psychoanalytic Study of the Child* (New York: International Universities Press, 1947), 2:34. The authors stress the development of the ego ideal during latency and adolescence and the great need for "conformity" if no clear-cut cultural values can supplement the older superego structure.

14. Ives Hendrick, "Instinct and the Ego during Infancy," *Psychoanalytic Quarterly* 9 (1942): 33–58.

15. Fenichel, *Psychoanalytic Theory of Neurosis*, p. 13.

16. Erwin Straus, "Die aufrechte Haltung: Eine anthropologische Studie," *Monatsschrift fuer Psychiatrie und Neurologie* 117 (1949): 367–79, trans. in *Psychiatric Quarterly* 26 (1952): 529.

17. Karl Buehler, *Die geistige Entwicklung des Kindes*, 2d ed. (Jena: G. Fischer, 1921), pp. 434 ff. K. Buehler has not actually coined this term but uses it in a meaning closer to the one we have in mind than have other psychologists.

18. G. F. Hegel, *Theologische Jugendschriften*, p. 380. Author's translation; quoted after L. Binswanger, *Grundformen und Erkenntnis menschlichen Daseins* (Zürich: Max Niehaus, 1942), p. 508.

19. Sigmund Freud, *Civilization and its Discontents*, trans. and ed. James Strachey (New York: W. W. Norton & Company, Inc., 1962), p. 85.

20. Theodor Reik, *Fragments of a Great Confession* (New York: Farrar Straus & Co., 1949), p. 385.

21. Alexander, *Fundamentals of Psychoanalysis*, pp. 50, 54.

22. Theodor Reik, *Masochism in Modern Man* (New York: Farrar & Rinehart, 1941), p. 115.

23. J. K. Friedjung, "Ueber verschiedene Quellen kindlicher Schamhaftigkeit," *Internationale Zeitschrift fuer Psychoanalyse* 1 (1913).

24. Personal communications.

Notes to Part II

1. Ruth Benedict, *The Chrysanthemum and the Sword* (Boston: Houghton Mifflin, 1946), pp. 222-24.
2. Margaret Mead, *Social Change and Cultural Surrogates*, reprinted with slight abridgment in Clyde Kluckhohn and Henry Murray, *Personality in Nature, Society and Culture* (New York: Alfred A. Knopf, 1948), pp. 511-22. Originally printed in *Journal of Educational Sociology* 14 (1940): 92-110. Erik H. Erikson, *Childhood and Society* (New York: W. W. Norton & Company, Inc., 1963), pp. 393-402. S. D. Clark, "Religion and Economic Backward Areas," *American Economic Review* 41 (1951). On the Weber thesis: Max Weber, *The Protestant Ethic and the Spirit of Capitalism*, trans. Talcott Parsons (New York: Charles Scribner's Sons, 1930). R. H. Tawney, *Religion and the Rise of Capitalism: A Historical Study* (New York: Harcourt, Brace and Company, 1926). Pelican Books Edition: New York: Penguin Books, Inc., 1949. Max Weber, *The Religion of China: Confucianism and Taoism*, trans. and ed. Hans H. Gerth (Glencoe, Ill.: The Free Press, 1951), especially chapter 8, "Conclusions: Confucianism and Puritanism."
3. A. L. Kroeber, *Anthropology* (New York: Harcourt, Brace and Company, 1948), p. 612.
4. Sigmund Freud, *Civilization and its Discontents*, trans. and ed. James Strachey (New York: W. W. Norton & Company, Inc., 1962). T. V. Smith, *Beyond Conscience* (New York and London: Whittlesey House, McGraw-Hill Book Company, Inc., 1934). Karen Horney, *The Neurotic Personality of Our Time* (New York: W. W. Norton & Company, Inc., 1937), especially chapters 13-15. Erich Fromm, *Escape from Freedom* (New York: Rinehart and Company, 1941. United Nations Educational, Scientific, and Cultural Organization, *Educational and Psychological Techniques for Changing Mental Attitudes Affecting International Understanding*, prepared by Anna Freud (SS/-TAIU/7), September 7, 1948. F. L. K. Hsu, "Suppression versus Repression," *Psychiatry* 12 (1949). David Riesman, Reuel Denney, and Nathan Glazer, *The Lonely Crowd: A Study of*

the Changing American Character (New Haven, Conn.: The Yale University Press, 1950).

5. Margaret Mead, ed., *Cooperation and Competition Among Primitive Peoples* (New York: McGraw-Hill Book Company, Inc., 1937), especially pp. 493–505, in the editor's "Interpretive Statement."

6. Margaret Mead, "Collective Guilt," *Proceedings of the International Congress on Mental Health, London, 1948*. Vol. 3. The distinction between internal and external sanctions is not prominent in this paper.

7. Laura Thompson and Alice Joseph, *The Hopi Way* (Chicago: University of Chicago Press, 1947). Gordon MacGregor, Royal B. Hassrich, and William E. Henry, *Warriors Without Weapons: A Study of the Society and Personality Development of the Pine Ridge Sioux* (Chicago: University of Chicago Press, 1946). Dorothea Leighton and Clyde Kluckhohn, *Children of the People: The Navaho Individual and His Development* (Cambridge: Harvard University Press, 1947). Alice Joseph, Rosamond B. Spicer, and Jane Chesky, *The Desert People: A Study of the Papago Indians* (Chicago: University of Chicago Press, 1949). I have also consulted several unpublished manuscripts by Robert Havighurst in which he presents and analyzes comparative data from the psychological tests. See fn. 15.

8. Leighton and Kluckhohn, *Children of the People*, pp. 170–71.

9. *Ibid.*, p. 170.

10. *Ibid.*, p. 106.

11. *Ibid.*

12. *Ibid.*

13. Kluckhohn and Leighton seem to oscillate between both of these extremes. The passage quoted from them on progress should be taken along with another passage where they point out that the Navaho disapprove of some of the same "wrong deeds" that the whites disapprove of, and conclude from this observation that "the differences are not one of presence or absence of 'moral standards,' but rather a different mechanism of enforcing these standards." *Ibid.*, p. 171.

14. W. E. Henry, *The Thematic Apperception Technique in the Study of Culture-Personality Relations* (Provincetown, Mass.: The Journal Press, 1947), p. 107. Published as a "separate" and in *Genetic Psychology Monographs* 35 (1947): 3–135.

15. The principal test data which I cite will be found in the following unpublished memoranda by Robert Havighurst, Committee on Human Development, University of Chicago.

a) "A Comparison of American Indian Children and White

Children by Means of the Emotional Response Test."

b) Supplement to same (a).

c) "The Moral Ideology of Indian Children of the Southwest and Sioux."

d) Revised version of same.

e) "The Attitudes of Navaho, Zuni, and Sioux Children toward Rules of Games."

f) Supplement to same.

g) "Belief in Immanent Justice and Animism among Indian Children of the Southwest and Sioux."

Selected samples from this data are also given in the published monographs on the different tribes.

16. Thompson and Joseph, *The Hopi Way*, pp. 102–3.

17. George A. Pettitt, *Primitive Education in North America* (Berkeley and Los Angeles: University of California Press, 1946).

18. Havighurst, "Moral Ideology."

19. Havighurst, "Immanent Justice." See also Margaret Mead, *Journal of the Royal Anthropological Institute* 52 (1932): 173–92.

20. In her paper "Collective Guilt" Margaret Mead offers a somewhat different interpretation of the relation of individual to collective responsibility. Another parallel between "the Protestant Ethic" of an Indian tribe and of Western Europe is drawn by Walter Goldschmidt, "Ethics and the Structure of Society: An Ethnological Contribution to the Sociology of Knowledge," *American Anthropologist* 53 (1951): 506–23.

21. The possibility that the test results may be closely related to the variety of words for "shame," "remorse," "guilt," etc., is also suggested by Havighurst "*A Comparison of Children*," p. 17.

22. A. I. Hallowell, "The Rorschach Technique in the Study of Personality and Culture," *American Anthropologist* 47 (April–June 1945). T. M. Abel and F. L. K. Hsu, "Some Aspects of Personality of Chinese as Revealed by the Rorschach Test," *Journal of Projective Techniques* 13 (1949).

23. D. Rappaport, *Diagnostic Psychological Testing*, 2 vols. (Chicago: Yearbook Publishers, 1945). Not only stresses the difficulty in deciding whether a test indication refers to a conscious overt trend or to an unconscious latent trend but states flatly that integration of the theory of ego psychology with that of observed thought patterns "is the great unresolved task of projective testing," p. 11.

24. A. I. Hallowell, "Fear and Anxiety as Cultural and Individual Variables in a Primitive Society," *Journal of Social Psychology* 9 (1938): 25–47. A. Irving Hallowell, "Aggression in Saulteaux Society," reprinted in *Personality in Nature, Society, and Cul-*

ture, eds. Clyde Kluckhohn and Henry A. Murray (New York: Alfred A. Knopf, 1948), pp. 204–19. Originally printed in *Psychiatry* 3 (1940): 395–407. A. Irving Hallowell, "The Social Function of Anxiety in a Primitive Society," in *Personal Character and Cultural Milieu*, rev. ed., ed. Douglas G. Haring (Syracuse, N.Y.: Syracuse University Press, 1949), pp. 375–88. Dorothy Eggan, "The General Problem of Hopi Adjustment," reprinted, with some revisions by the author, in *Personality*, eds. Kluckhohn and Murray, pp. 220–35. Originally published in *American Anthropologist* 45 (1943): 357–73. Donald Horton, "The Functions of Alcohol in Primitive Societies: A Cross-Cultural Study," reprinted in part, with revisions by the author, in *Personality*, eds. Kluckhohn and Murray, pp. 540–50. Originally published in *The Quarterly Journal of Studies in Alcohol* 4 (1943): 292–303. Esther Goldfrank, "Socialization, Personality and the Structure of Pueblo Society," reprinted in *Personal Character*, ed. Haring. Originally printed in *American Anthropologist* 47 (1945): 516, 539. Anna Freud, *op. cit.*

25. A good measure of this transformation is given in Kroeber's two reviews of *Totem and Taboo*, the first published in 1920 in the *American Anthropologist* and the second in 1939 in the *American Journal of Sociology*.

26. G. Róheim, "The Study of Character Development and the Ontogenetic Theory of Culture," in *Essays Presented to C. G. Seligman* and *Psychoanalysis and Anthropology* (New York: International Universities Press, 1951).

27. B. Malinowski, *Sex and Repression in Savage Society* (London: Routledge and Kegan Paul Ltd., 1927).

28. A. Kardiner and R. Linton, *The Individual and His Society* (New York: Columbia University Press, 1939) and A. Kardiner *et al.*, *The Psychological Frontiers of Society* (New York: Columbia University Press, 1945).

29. Margaret Mead, "The Study of National Character," in *The Policy Sciences*, eds. Daniel Lerner and Harold D. Lasswell (Stanford, Calif.: Stanford University Press, 1951).

30. Robert Redfield, "The Primitive World View," *Proceedings of the American Philosophical Society* 96 (February 21, 1952). See also his *The Primitive World and its Transformations* (Ithaca, N.Y.: Cornell University Press, 1957).

31. See, e.g., R. Pettazzoni, "Confession of Sins in Primitive Cultures," *Papers and Transcript of the Jubilee Congress of the Folk-lore Society, London, 1930*, pp. 176–81.

INDEX

Index

Index